Don't Forget Us!

I · COME · FROM

ROMANIA

Anita Ganeri

A Watts Book

LONDON · NEW YORK · SYDNEY

© Aladdin Books Ltd 1995
Designed and produced by
Aladdin Books Ltd
28 Percy Street
London W1P 9FF

First published in
Great Britain in 1995 by
Watts Books
96 Leonard Street
London EC2A 4RH

Editor: Jim Pipe
Designer: Pete Bennett
Illustrator: David Burroughs
Consultant: Michael Lee
Photo
Research: Brooks Krikler
               Research

Printed in Belgium
A CIP catalogue record for this
book is available from the
British Library.

ISBN 0 7496 1859 0

CONTENTS

INTRODUCTION

Hello! My name is Mariana and I come from Romania. I was born in Bucharest, the capital city of my country. Today, though, I live in the West with my parents and my sister, Liliana, and brother, Alexandru. My family left Romania because they did not agree with the very strict way the Communist government used to rule.

Though the Communist government has gone now, life remains just as hard for many Romanians. However, one day I would like to return, even though I have made lots of friends here. Let me tell you about my old home and what it is like to live there.

Under Communist rule, it was very difficult for people to leave Romania. They had to get permission from the government to travel anywhere. People sometimes managed to defect, or escape, from Romania. It was a brave thing to do because, at that time, they did not expect to see their homes or families again. Today, though the new government in power has given people more freedom, many strict laws remain.

ROMANIA TODAY

Romania is a country in southeastern Europe. It lies to the north of the Balkan Peninsula, a mountainous region which includes all or part of the countries of Albania, Bulgaria, Greece, Turkey, Romania and the former Yugoslavia. Romania covers an area of 237,500 sq km, about half the size of Spain. It has land borders with Hungary, Bulgaria, the former Yugoslavia, Moldova and the Ukraine.

Romania also has a long coastline in the east, along the Black Sea. Most of its land borders follow the course of rivers, such as the Danube. Romania itself is divided into 40 counties and the special district of Bucharest.

Salut

(Left) Almost everyone in Romania speaks the Romanian language. Here you can see the Romanian word for 'Hello'!

(Right) A typical village scene in Romania, with the local Orthodox Church in the background.

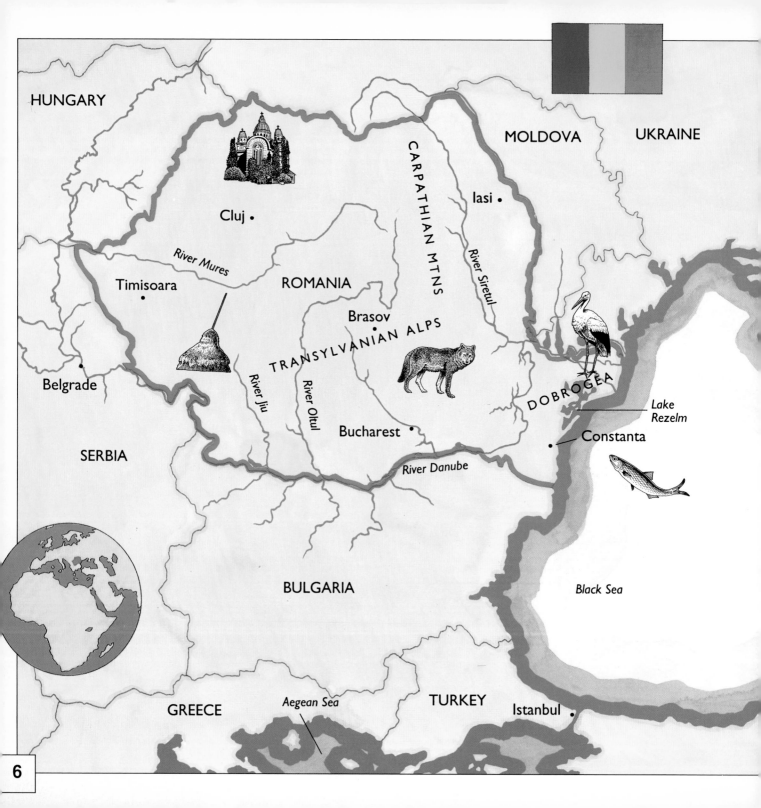

HUNGARY

MOLDOVA

UKRAINE

Cluj •

Iasi •

River Mures

CARPATHIAN MTNS

River Siretul

ROMANIA

Timisoara

Brasov

TRANSYLVANIAN ALPS

River Jiu

River Oltul

Belgrade

DOBROGEA

Lake
Rezelm

Bucharest

Constanta

SERBIA

River Danube

BULGARIA

Black Sea

GREECE

Aegean Sea

TURKEY

Istanbul •

6

COUNTRY AND CLIMATE

A curving chain of mountains runs through the north and centre of Romania. They are all part of the Carpathian mountain system. Mount Moldoveanu (2,543 m high) in the Transylvanian Alps (the Southern Carpathians) is the highest mountain in Romania. The slopes of the mountains are covered in thick forests. Huge, fertile plains lie around them. These have the best farmland and most of Romania's cities and towns.

The River Danube is the longest and most important river in Romania. It flows 1,400 km south and then west across Romania. There are also thousands of small lakes, many of them high up in the mountains. Romania has hot, sunny summers and cold, snowy winters.

The River Danube (right) flows into the Black Sea through a huge, triangular-shaped delta in north Romania. The delta changes shape and size as the river deposits more mud and silt. This area is famous for its wildlife, such as pelicans and storks.

LAND OF THE ROMANS

In the 4th century BC, a people called the Dacians lived in the area which is now Romania. In 106 AD, the Romans invaded Dacia and the area became known as Romania, meaning "land of the Romans". The Romans introduced Christianity to the region, and later Romania joined the Orthodox Church after the split with the Catholic Church. (The Orthodox Sihastre monastery, right, dates from 1724.)

For the next 800 years, Romania was invaded many times by the Goth, Hun, Avar, Slav and Bulgar tribes. In the 1300s, Romania became part of the Turkish Ottoman Empire. Many Romanian princes and nobles fought against Turkish rule but it was not until 1878 that Romania became an independent kingdom ruled over by King Carol I.

The Romans conquered Dacia under the Emperor Trajan. He celebrated by having a victory column built in Rome. The carvings on Trajan's Column show the Roman troops fighting the Dacians (left).

THE PEOPLE OF ROMANIA

Some 23 million people live in Romania, about half as many as live in Britain or France. My family and the vast majority of people are Romanians descended from the original Dacians, who mixed with Romans and the various tribes of invaders. Throughout history, however, Romania has also been home to a wide variety of ethnic groups.

Parts of Transylvania are heavily populated with Hungarians and Germans who arrived in the 12th century. Later, Turks and Ukrainians settled along the Black Sea Coast and in the Dobrogea region. There were once thousands of Gypsies, or *Romanies*, wandering through Romania. Today there are far fewer but their colourful, lively folk culture, dances and music are still going strong.

One of the most famous Romanians of modern times was the sculptor, Constantin Brancusi (1876-1957). He studied in Paris where he was influenced by the great French sculptor, Rodin. Brancusi (right) was best known for the way he gave life and character to simple shapes and forms.

Old and new: this girl (above) is wearing an old-style waistcoat over a modern machine-knitted jumper.

(Top right) A Gypsy boy wearing a sheepskin cloak with his trainers.

(Right) This Carpathian huntsman keeps his head warm with a traditional hat!

DAILY LIFE

I used to live with my family in a small flat in Bucharest. Like many people in Romania, my family was quite poor. In the West, almost everyone seems to have a television and a car. In Romania, very few people can afford these luxuries. Our family used to get up early in the morning to be ready for work or school at 8am. In the evening, the whole family gathered for our main meal. Then we had to do our homework before we went to bed.

Under Communist rule, life was very hard indeed for ordinary people. The government had great power over our lives and controlled our jobs, schools, religion and so on. After the fall of the Communists in 1989, the new leaders tried to make it easier for Romanians to earn a living, but Western goods are still too expensive for most people.

Special events, such as weddings and christenings, are celebrated in grand style. People wear colourful, traditional costumes and dance and play music. In the countryside, there are also special festivals every year to celebrate important events, such as the harvest.

(Above) This woman from the town of Cluj is delighted at her new pots. Many goods in Romania continue to be in short supply and long queues can be seen outside most shops.

(Right) Gypsies are a nomadic people who live in small villages and in the outskirts of towns and cities. Many gypsies cannot find work and as a result live in bad conditions and cannot afford to eat properly.

FOOD AND DRINK

Romanian food is not very well known in the West, so let me introduce you to it! There are some delicious dishes. Romanian specialities include *mititei* (grilled meatballs), *brinzec* (cheese snacks) and *patricieni* (sausages). You can buy these from street stalls. We also eat *mamaliga* (a sort of thick porridge made from corn flour), often with *sarmale* (stuffed cabbage leaves) or *tocana* (a stew made with pork, garlic and onions). We also like sweet things, such as cakes, pastries and doughnuts, and special treats, such as cheese pancakes and plum dumplings. *Papanasi* are doughnuts made with cream and cheese.

Popular drinks for adults include red or white Romanian wines, which come from the Dobrogea and Danube regions. *Tzuica*, a type of strong plum brandy, is another favourite. People drink this hot in the cold weather to warm them up!

Depiste reforms by the new government, people still spend many hours queuing, even for basic foods like bread and milk.

(Top right) This woman is using a coal-burning oven to cook her *tocana* (stew).

Romanians buy food from shops in town or from markets in the street. But we do not have such well stocked shops as those in western Europe and North America. A stall from London (above) displays exotic fruit from around the world, while the typical Romanian market (right) relies on locally-grown goods such as cabbages and pickled vegetables.

(Left) In the Romanian Orthodox Church, part of the service is a combination of a confession of sins with a communion. The priest lays his cloth over the communicant, and reads passages from the Bible. Meanwhile he touches the communicant on the head with his crucifix.

OUR BELIEFS

The Communist government did not encourage people to follow a faith. They did not tell us not to go to church, but made sure that people who went were punished in some way. They might not be promoted at work, for example. Today, people are free to worship whenever and wherever they wish. Three-quarters of people are Christians, belonging to the Romanian Orthodox Church.

Most Hungarians and Germans living in Romania are Roman Catholics or Protestants, while Turks in the country are usually Muslims. There are also a small number of Jews. There are a large number of churches and monasteries in Romania (priests, reading from the Bible, are shown left). Many churches are very old and beautifully decorated inside and out.

(Right) Icons are paintings on wood of saints or of holy figures such as Mary and Jesus. You will see lots of them in an Orthodox church. People use them to help them pray and to meditate.

SCHOOL AND WORK

In Romania, we have to go to school from the ages of six to 16. We spend eight years at primary school, then take an exam to go to secondary school. Some pupils study arts subjects (literature, languages and history). Others study science subjects (maths, physics and computing). After four years at secondary school, we take a school-leaving examination, called the *baccalaureate* (as in France). Then some students go to college or university; others start work.

Many people work in factories (as my father used to), making machinery, chemicals, iron and steel (left). The Communist government used to own all the factories in Romania and wages were very low. Though many factories are now owned by individuals, factory workers still earn only about a thirtieth of the amount earned by factory workers in western European countries and the United States.

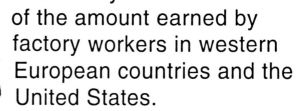

In the past, most people in Romania worked as farmers. Many people still farm the land but more and more have moved to the cities to find jobs in industry.

CITY LIFE

About half of the Romanian people live in towns and cities. Bucharest, where my family used to live, is the capital of Romania and is its biggest city by far. Some 2 million people live in Bucharest. The city was badly damaged by bombs in World War II but some of its old buildings, including many churches, survived. (If you look carefully at the picture on the right, you can see some of these in the distance.) There is a wide main avenue, like the Champs Elysées in Paris, where people like to stroll and have a drink at the street-side cafes.

In contrast to the old buildings of the city, many modern buildings were put up in Communist times. Most city people live in small flats in modern, high-rise blocks. The cities are growing fast and there are often shortages of houses for people.

Bucharest is the centre of Romania's transport system. The city has an international airport and is the centre of the road and rail networks. Very few people can afford to buy their own cars. In the city itself, people usually travel by tram or bus, which can get very crowded (right)!

LIFE IN THE VILLAGES

Life is much slower and more traditional in the villages which dot the Romanian countryside. People live in simple cottages, decorated with hand-made rugs, carved wooden furniture and hand-painted plates. They have a vegetable plot where they grow food for their families. Many villagers on the plains work as farmers, growing corn, barley, potatoes, sugar beet, grapes and other fruit. In the mountains, farmers herd sheep and goats (left). The Communists organised all the farms into huge, collective farms which were worked by hundreds of families. Today, these are being broken up into smaller, privately-owned farms again.

There are fishing villages all around the Danube Delta. The delta provides about half of all Romania's fish (see local fishermen, left). This includes sturgeon, which is highly valued for its roe (called caviar), mackerel and mullet. Reeds are also harvested to make paper.

Thick forests cover the mountain slopes. They provide valuable timber and are also the home of many wild animals, including bears.

SPORT AND LEISURE

Romanian people do not have much spare time or money left over for hobbies or leisure activities. At the weekend, people go to the park or cinema if they live in a town, or sit outside and chat to their friends in the countryside. We also like to listen to pop music. The two favourite holiday spots for Romanians are the mountains and the Black Sea coast (top right). You can walk, climb and ski in the mountains or visit some of the ancient castles, including one which is said to have been the home of Count Dracula (top far right)! He was actually a Romanian prince, called Vlad the Impaler.

Football is the most popular spectator sport in Romania. Fans follow the national team with great interest (bottom right). Romania reached the quarter-finals of the 1994 World Cup in the USA.

Many champion gymnasts have come from Romania, including Nadia Comaneci (left). At the 1976 Olympic Games, she became the first gymnast ever to be awarded a perfect 10 mark. In 1989, Nadia Comaneci defected (escaped) from Romania and fled to Austria. She later went to live in the USA.

WHY I'M HERE

The Communists came to power in Romania in the 1940s, at the end of World War II. At first, the government followed the wishes of the former USSR but later set up their own policies. These policies made life very difficult for ordinary people. People had very little freedom and were terrified of being reported to the government by the Securitate, or secret police. In the late 1980s, Communist governments in other countries, such as Poland and the USSR were overthrown. In 1989, thousands of Romanians took to the streets to rebel against the harshness of Ceaucescu's rule (right). Many people were arrested or killed, but the revolution did succeed in overthrowing the government. My parents had to leave Romania just before this. Otherwise they might have been arrested too.

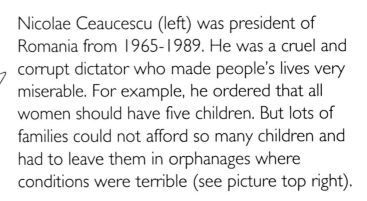

Nicolae Ceaucescu (left) was president of Romania from 1965-1989. He was a cruel and corrupt dictator who made people's lives very miserable. For example, he ordered that all women should have five children. But lots of families could not afford so many children and had to leave them in orphanages where conditions were terrible (see picture top right).

The Romanian government elected in 1990 asked Romanian miners (below) to attack those who disagreed with its policies. Many feel that, despite its reforms, the government has not done enough to improve the lives of the Romanian people since Ceaucescu's fall.

MY FUTURE

After the revolution in 1989, people in Romania were overjoyed to see the end of Nicolae Ceaucescu and the Communist government. Free, multi-party elections were held in Romania in 1990 and a non-Communist government elected. But many of the ministers and officials had previously been members of the Communist party and many people were suspicious of them.

Since the elections, Romanians have had more freedom in their lives. They can now travel and worship freely. However, there is a long way to go. Most people are still very poor and there are problems with rising prices, low wages and unemployment. Romania is adjusting, slowly but surely, to its new situation and one day I hope that I can go back there with my family. Then I can tell my friends in Romania all about my other home in the West.

Goodbye (La revedere)!

FACT FILE

Official name: Republica România (Republic of Romania)

National language: Romanian

Other languages: Hungarian, German

Population: 23 million

Currency: Leu (plural *lei*)

Form of government: Multi-party Republic

Head of state: President

Capital city: Bucharest

Other major cities: Cluj, Timisoara, Brasov, and Constanta

Area: 237,500 square kilometres

Main religions: Romanian Orthodox (75%), Roman Catholic (7%). Also some Protestants, Jews and Muslims

Ethnic groups: Romanians (85%), Hungarians (8%), Germans (2%), also Gypsies, Turks, Ukrainians

Climate: Continental

Major rivers: Danube, Jiu, Oltul, Arges, Siretul, Prat

Highest mountain: Mt Moldoveanu (2,543 metres above sea level)

Crops: Maize, wheat, grapes and other fruits, potatoes, sugar beet

Mineral resources: Natural gas, petroleum, bauxite, coal, copper, gold, iron ore, silver, lead silver, zinc

Industries: Machinery, mining, cement, iron and steel, petroleum and wood products, food processing, clothing, footwear

Major exports: Industrial machinery, fuels, chemicals, cement, clothing, shoes, processed foods, timber

Major imports: Industrial machinery, iron ore, chemicals, fuels, coal, cotton

INDEX

Photocredits:
Special thanks to Frank Spooner Pictures for supplying all the pictures in this book
apart from the following pages: Cover inset, 3, 15 top left, 29: Roger Vlitos; 21: Panos
Pictures; 24 top left: Topham Picture Point.